CHARACTER GUIDE

FANTASTIC BEASTS

AND WHERE TO FIND THEM™

CHARACTER GUIDE

BY MICHAEL KOGGE

SCHOLASTIC INC.

www.fantasticbeasts.com

ISBN 978-1-338-11678-6

10 9 8 7 6 5 4 3 2 1   16 17 18 19 20

Printed in the U.S.A.   23

First printing 2016

Art Direction: Rick DeMonico
Page Design: Two Red Shoes Design

CONTENTS

INTRODUCTION

Newt Scamander, the world's preeminent Magizoologist, strongly believes that magical beasts should be studied and protected. Newt has made this his life's mission, traveling the globe to carry out his research.

The adventure begins when Newt arrives in New York City in the winter of 1926, with nothing more in his possession than the clothes on his back and one modest leather case. But his is no ordinary case—it is the magical home of a fantastic array of wild beasts!

Jacob Kowalski—who is referred to by the American wizarding community as a No-Maj because he does not have magical powers—meets Newt when they are both at a local bank. Following a misunderstanding, Jacob and Newt get into a skirmish outside the bank, and the two accidentally switch cases. Jacob gets the surprise of his life when he returns home and opens Newt's case, unwittingly unleashing many of the Magizoologist's beloved beasts.

Meanwhile, there is something dark and ferocious terrorizing New York City. It's crushing cars, blasting through walls, and shattering windows. Some No-Majs explain the unusual disturbances as strange weather, but others suspect the truth: Dark magic is afoot. Mary Lou Barebone, the leader of the New Salem Philanthropic Society, leads a vocal charge in alerting people about what she believes is sinister witchcraft and wizardry all around them. Her ultimate goal is to stamp out magic through a new round of Salem Witch Trials.

As Newt searches the city for his runaway beasts, he becomes further entangled not only with Jacob, but also with two witch sisters named Tina and Queenie Goldstein, who work for the Magical Congress of the United States of America, MACUSA. Once the Congress becomes aware of Newt's escaped creatures, they blame him for the troubles in the city.

Newt tries unsuccessfully to convince MACUSA that his beasts are innocent. He has seen this kind of carnage before, and believes it to be the sign of an Obscurus—a dark and violent force that manifests itself when a child born with magical powers suppresses his or her abilities. But MACUSA refuses to believe that an Obscurus in New York City could even be a possibility. There hasn't been one in North America in over 200 years, since American witches and wizards began practicing magic in secret.

How can Newt save himself—and his beasts—if no one will listen to the truth?

NEWT
SCAMANDER

CHARACTER OVERVIEW

NAME:
NEWTON ("NEWT") ARTEMIS FIDO SCAMANDER

PROFESSION:
MAGIZOOLOGIST

SCHOOLING:
HOGWARTS SCHOOL OF WITCHCRAFT AND WIZARDRY

KEEN OBSERVER

Newt has a scientist's eye for detail, regularly spotting odd minutiae that others overlook. Newt has a thirst for knowledge about magical creatures, and his main objective is to protect them and educate others about them. However, this often gets him into serious trouble.

INTELLIGENT INTROVERT

No problem is ever too difficult, and no situation is ever too hopeless for Newt. His mind is always inventing solutions that, as far-fetched as they seem, often end up saving the day. He's not a particularly chatty man and rarely wastes time explaining what he's thinking or doing—much to the worry of nervous companions like Jacob Kowalski, the No-Maj that gets caught up in Newt's adventures in New York City.

INTREPID EXPLORER

Fearless to the point of foolhardiness, Newt strides—or bumbles—straight into the heart of danger, particularly if it involves a mysterious species. The legendary creatures that terrify witches, wizards, and No-Majs alike fascinate Newt, and he has traveled all around the globe to study and document them.

CLOTHING & POSSESSIONS

GREATCOAT

The signature piece of Newt's wardrobe is his single-breasted, peacock-blue overcoat. It is close-fitting, and covers his body down to his knees.

SUIT

Under his overcoat, Newt wears a dark brown suit jacket and pants.

WAISTCOAT

The burnt-orange waistcoat adds a splash of color to Newt's attire.

SHIRT

Newt wears an ivory-white shirt.

BOW TIE

Newt's bow tie is fashioned out of strips of treated cloth.

BOOTS

Newt's calf-high leather boots are weather-beaten and worn from his travels across the world.

POCKETS

The many pockets in Newt's coats are seemingly bottomless, carrying an untold number of possessions.

Pickett is a tiny Bowtruckle, a twig-like magical beast, who resides behind the lapel of Newt's greatcoat. This beast pretends to be sick because he likes being close to Newt.

Newt also keeps a Swooping Evil in his pocket. This beast looks like a small, spiny, green cocoon, but when tossed like a skipping stone, it unfurls into a stunning, giant, winged creature— much like an oversized butterfly.

Potions and elixirs can often be found in Newt's pockets. As a Magizoologist, Newt must be prepared for anything.

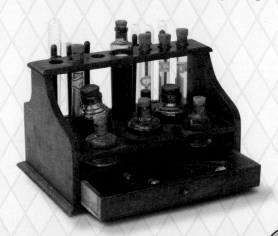

CLOTHING & POSSESSIONS

SCARF

Sometimes Newt drapes a black-and-yellow wool scarf, the colors of Hufflepuff house, his Hogwarts home, over his neck for greater warmth in the chilly New York weather.

WAND

More organic in appearance than many wands, the end of Newt's wand still bears some of its original tree bark.

LEATHER CASE

If the lock on Newt's case is set to "Muggle Worthy," all that will be visible within are typical No-Maj wares, like clothing, an alarm clock, and binoculars. When not on this setting, the case opens up into an expansive world of specialized habitats for each of his fantastic beasts.

FANTASTIC BEASTS AND WHERE TO FIND THEM

Newt spent a year in Equatorial Guinea writing this still-unfinished manuscript to educate readers on magical creatures and the need to preserve and protect them.

CHARACTER PHILOSOPHY

TRUTH CHASER

While most other witches and wizards have doubted the existence of a certain beast, Newt locates it with a singular passion, going after every lead, no matter how preposterous.

LIVING IN THE PRESENT

Newt doesn't just admire magical creatures; he loves their zest for living in the present. He tries to follow their example, enjoying what each moment brings, not being frightened by death.

> "MY PHILOSOPHY IS: WORRYING MEANS YOU SUFFER TWICE."
>
> –Newt Scamander

MAGIC

As a Magizoologist, Newt's talents include caring for and protecting beasts, yet he's also well versed in spells across wizarding disciplines.

ABERTO

This spell opens portals of all kinds. Newt uses this spell to open the vault doors housing the safe at Steen National Bank while he's trying to catch an escaped Niffler, a small beast attracted to shiny objects.

ACCIO

This charm brings a person, place, or thing closer to the caster. The Niffler is determined to pocket as much shiny loot as possible, and keeps escaping despite Newt's attempts to summon the beast into his hand.

ECHOLOCATION
ECHO-DETECTION CHARMS

Ripples of force emanate and rebound. Newt uses echolocation to locate his missing beasts. When the beasts are detected, the ripples rebound back in Newt's direction, letting him know he's on the right track.

REPARO

This spell mends broken physical objects and returns them to their original state. Newt undoes some of the mess left behind by the Niffler by repairing the pieces of a shattered jewelry store window in New York City's Diamond District.

STUPEFY

This charm momentarily dazes a person or group of people. Newt casts this spell while trying to break into the vault at Steen National Bank. It works—the guards drop to the floor, stunned.

BACKGROUND

BATTLE DAMAGE

In apprehending his magical beasts, Newt admits he's suffered a "few nips" over the years.

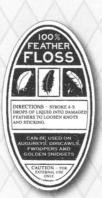

100% FEATHER FLOSS

DIRECTIONS ~ STROKE 4-5 DROPS OF LIQUID INTO DAMAGED FEATHERS TO LOOSEN KNOTS AND STICKING.

CAN BE USED ON AUGUREYS, DIRICAWLS, FWOOPERS AND GOLDEN SNIDGETS

CAUTION ~ FOR EXTERNAL USE ONLY.

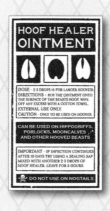

HOOF HEALER OINTMENT

DOSE - 2-3 DROPS (6 FOR LARGER HOOVES).
DIRECTIONS - RUB THE OINTMENT ONTO THE SURFACE OF THE BEASTS HOOF. WIPE OFF ANY EXCESS WITH A COTTON TOWEL. EXTERNAL USE ONLY.
CAUTION - ONLY TO BE USED ON HOOVES.

CAN BE USED ON HIPPOGRIFFS, PORLOCKS, MOONCALVES AND OTHER HOOVED BEASTS

IMPORTANT - IF INFECTION CONTINUES AFTER 10 DAYS TRY USING A SEALING SAP MIXED WITH ANOTHER 2-3 DROPS OF HOOF HEALER. LEAVE FOR 3 HOURS.

☠ DO NOT USE ON NOGTAILS.

SHELL SHINER

DIRECTIONS
SHAKE WELL BEFORE USING.
RUB LIQUID INTO SHELL USING A DAMP CLOTH. FOR BETTER SHINE RUB OFF USING A DRY COTTON CLOTH IN CLOCKWISE MOTIONS.

DOSAGE
FOR LARGER SHELLS .... 3-5 DROPS
FOR MEDIUM SHELLS .... 2-3 DROPS
FOR SMALLER SHELLS .... 1-2 DROPS

CAN BE USED ON FIRE CRABS, MACKLED MALACLAWS, STREELERS AND ALL OTHER SHELLED CREATURES

INGREDIENTS
DITTANY .... 1 FLUID OZ.
WORMWOOD .... 1 1/2 FLUID OZ.
SALT WATER .... 6 FLUID OZ.

☐ DO NOT USE ON NEW BORN BEASTS
☐ STRICTLY FOR EXTERNAL USE ONLY

BEAK BALM

DIRECTIONS - RUB A TEASPOON FULL OF BALM ON DAMAGED AREA OF BEAK. APPLY EVERY HOUR.
IF INFECTION CONTINUES AFTER 10 DAYS TRY MIXING WITH A SALT SERUM.

CAN BE USED ON AUGUREYS, DIRICAWLS, FWOOPERS AND OTHER BEAKED CREATURES

CAUTION - DO NOT USE ON GRIFFIN OR HIPPOGRIFF BEAKS.

HEALTHY HORN POLISH

DIRECTIONS-
POUR 2-3 DROPS OF POLISH ONTO A DAMP CLOTH AND RUB INTO BEASTS HORN. RUB OFF ANY EXCESS WITH A DRY TOWEL.

CAUTION-
DO NOT USE ON INFECTED HORNS.

PERFECT FOR ERUMPENT, GRAPHORN, RE'EM AND TEBO HORNS.

EXTERNAL USE ONLY

SCALE SAP

DIRECTIONS - RUB A HANDFUL OF SAP INTO DAMAGED OR DRY SCALES. APPLY 3 TIMES A DAY.
DO NOT CONTINUE TO USE AFTER 10 DAYS.
CAUTION - DO NOT USE ON OPEN WOUNDS.

CAN BE USED ON MOKES AND RUNESPOORS. ALSO EFFECTIVE ON FISH SCALES.

IMPORTANT - DO NOT USE ON DRAGON OR SALAMANDER SCALES.

DRAGON MASTER

Like most young British men of his generation, Newt fought in the Great War, serving on the Eastern Front for the Ministry of Magic. He was enrolled in a top-secret program for handling dragons, most notably Ukrainian Ironbellies.

RELATIONSHIPS

TINA GOLDSTEIN

At first, Newt finds this former MACUSA Auror bothersome because she berates him for breaking the International Statute of Wizarding Secrecy. But over the course of a few days, Newt becomes more than fast friends with Tina.

JACOB KOWALSKI

A chance run-in between Newt and this Polish No-Maj at Steen National Bank turned into an accidental friendship. "Mr. Kowalski," as Newt sometimes calls him, proves to be of great assistance in locating the beasts who have escaped Newt's case.

DEFINING MOMENTS

BIG APPLE

When he arrives in customs, Newt has no idea what an adventure he is about to have in New York City.

HARD KNOCKS

While trying to catch the Niffler, Newt attracts an unwanted No-Maj companion, Jacob Kowalski. Before Newt can obliviate Jacob's memory of the magical events he witnessed, Jacob grabs Newt's case and strikes him with it. Not only does Jacob get away, he also mistakenly takes Newt's case, which contains the Magizoologist's marvelous beasts.

WRONGLY ACCUSED

Newt is hauled in front of the International Confederation at MACUSA to explain all the chaos that has been taking place since his arrival in New York. The delegation blames Newt's beasts for the horrible attacks around the city, but Newt insists that his beasts are harmless. President Seraphina Picquery gives Newt an infraction, and sends him to Graves for sentencing. Tina, seen by the president as an accessory to Newt, is sent with him. Graves chooses to sentence both Newt and Tina to death.

NOISY NEWT

Newt talks to beasts as if they were family, not creatures, and does not hesitate to do what is necessary to get their attention. In the case of the Erumpent, a giant beast with a tough hide and a dangerous horn, that means he has to lure her back into the safety of his case by acting like an Erumpent himself and doing a mating dance. This includes running around, stamping his feet, and bellowing at the top of his lungs.

TINA
GOLDSTEIN

NAME:
PORPENTINA ("TINA") GOLDSTEIN

PROFESSION:
MACUSA WAND PERMIT OFFICIAL (FORMER AUROR)

SCHOOLING:
ILVERMORNY SCHOOL OF WITCHCRAFT AND WIZARDRY

NEW YORK NATIVE

Tina can slip in and out of crowds without her fellow New Yorkers taking note. She occupies her time with street investigations of interesting cases like the Second Salemers, an anti-witchcraft group stirring up trouble for the wizarding community.

CLOTHING & POSSESSIONS

Tina pays no attention to the fashion trends that her sister, Queenie, so diligently follows. Practicality dictates what Tina wears—along with whatever she has in her closet.

HAT

Tina wears an unadorned gumdrop-shaped hat with an upturned brim that slopes down to cover her ears.

OVERCOAT

Tina wears an oversized, storm-colored coat with the collar pushed up to protect her neck and shroud her face when she's sleuthing.

UNDERCOAT

A gray double-breasted jacket provides Tina with an additional layer of defense against the cold.

BLOUSE

Under her thick coats, Tina's loose, white blouse is nondescript and forgettable—the perfect piece for a street investigator who wants to blend in.

PENDANT

Tina wears a golden locket that dangles from a long chain around her neck.

SLACKS

Tina wears her pants loose, as is the custom for the 1920s in New York City.

SHOES

Dark brown leather shoes with soft soles muffle Tina's footfalls when she needs to be inconspicuous.

CHARACTER PHILOSOPHY

RULE BREAKER

Despite being such a stickler for the rules, Tina bends them when she sees a greater purpose. MACUSA banned her from conducting investigations, yet Tina continues to go out on criminal probes as if she were still an Auror.

DOGGED DETERMINATION

When Tina sets her mind on something, she follows it through. She feels a steadfast drive for the truth, despite the inherent danger or risk to her career.

JUSTICE FOR ALL

Tina wants to keep the peace between the magical and No-Maj societies. As an Auror, she investigated both major and minor violations of the International Statute of Wizarding Secrecy. Even after losing her commission, she still doesn't hold in high regard wizards who seem to blatantly snub the law, like Newt Scamander.

"THAT'S A SECTION 3-A VIOLATION OF THE CODE!"

–Tina Goldstein

CHANGE OF HEART

Tina is dismayed when she first meets Newt and learns about the creatures in his case. But as she comes to know Newt and his beasts, she makes a complete shift, and comes to see how beautiful they are, and how much they need help.

MAGIC

Tina knows lots of spells, but she especially excels in charms that enhance her investigative skills.

OBLIVIATE

This charm erases specific memories, such as magical events, from a person's mind. Tina scolds Newt for not Obliviating Jacob Kowalski, a No-Maj who saw him do magic.

WAND

Tina casts spells with a standard wooden wand that fits her
no-frills nature.

BACKGROUND

DIFFICULT CHILDHOOD

When they were young, Tina and Queenie lost their parents to dragon pox.

DEMOTED

MACUSA stripped Tina of her title as Auror, and demoted her to work in the Wand Permit Office in the basement.

STUBBORN SURVEILLANCE

The fact that she's no longer an Auror hasn't stopped Tina from continuing her surveillance of the New Salem Philanthropic Society. She regularly attends their rallies, despite having been instructed not to do so.

HIGH ALERT

Other than her locket, the only other shiny accessory Tina wears is a silver device around her wrist called an Admonitor. This magical tracker glows red at troublesome times.

RELATIONSHIPS

QUEENIE GOLDSTEIN

The two Goldstein sisters couldn't be more different, yet they are entirely devoted to each other. Since they were orphaned at an early age, Tina has often played mother to Queenie, acting as the authority figure. Nowadays, the relationship can seem reversed.

NEWT SCAMANDER

Tina has only known Newt for a short time, but the young Magizoologist has already made a big impression on her. Initially wary of Newt and his cavalier attitude toward the law, Tina warms to his unconventional ways, and finds him to be a wizard of much greater integrity and compassion than she originally anticipated.

SERAPHINA PICQUERY

The President of MACUSA and Tina don't see eye to eye about how Tina conducts herself professionally, which led to the latter losing her job as Auror. Tina thinks that if she can prove her worth to the organization again, they may reinstate her in her former role.

GNARLAK

Tina finds a questionable ally in the goblin owner of The Blind Pig, a lively bar where magical people congregate. Gnarlak provides her with information about New York's criminal magic underground—for the right price, of course.

DEFINING MOMENTS

CASE CLOSED

Tina brings Newt's magical case before the International Confederation of Witches and Wizards at MACUSA, which is currently in session because of the chaos in New York City. Tina tells those assembled that the fantastic creatures stored inside Newt's case have escaped and are causing mayhem in the city. Seraphina orders Tina to open the case. Tina knocks on the case, and Newt and Jacob climb out into the great hall.

SHOPPING SPREE

Tina assists Newt in tracking down a Demiguise named Dougal in a multi-floor department store. The search is all the more difficult since this long-haired, monkey-like beast has the ability to become invisible.

FRIENDLY FAREWELL

In the end, Newt leaves New York to go back to writing his book. Newt and Tina share a tender good-bye next to the steamer that will take Newt back home.

QUEENIE GOLDSTEIN

NAME:
QUEENIE GOLDSTEIN

PROFESSION:
MACUSA WAND PERMIT OFFICIAL

SCHOOLING:
ILVERMORNY SCHOOL OF WITCHCRAFT AND WIZARDRY

READY FOR ANYTHING

When her friends and family are in danger, Queenie proves she is brave, bold, and decisive.

CLOTHING & POSSESSIONS

Queenie loves wearing fashionable clothing. In addition to wearing a pink slip and pink pajamas around the house, she also wears a stylish pink ensemble when out and about the city.

COAT

Made of blush-colored silk with puffy lapels and cuffs, Queenie cuts a glamorous figure striding through the streets of New York. The coat's complementary collar provides Queenie with an extra dash of style.

SHOES

Queenie wears fashionable high heels regularly—even when on a mission.

WAND

Queenie's wand is the perfect merging of function and fashion: a black wand with a pearlescent shell handle.

FREE SPIRIT

Queenie enjoys all that life has to offer, finding pleasure in simple things like sewing and cooking.

SOUL

Queenie is a dreamer and wants to surround herself with beauty and excitement. She doesn't like the bleak basement of MACUSA where she works with her sister, Tina.

TREND TRACKER

A collector of wizarding fashion magazines, Queenie follows the ins and outs of popular culture.

SOCIAL SAVIOR FAIRE

Queenie doesn't need magic to work her special charm on other witches, wizards, or No-Majs. Her magnetism compels others to want to be near her.

MAGIC

Queenie is well versed in spells that make mundane tasks around the house a snap.

✳ ✳ ✳ ✳ ✳ ✳ ✳ 🦋 ✳ ✳ ✳ ✳ ✳ ✳ ✳

COOKING

With just a flick of her wand, Queenie can open kitchen cabinets, set the table, ready ingredients, and prepare a sumptuous meal.

STRONG SISTERS

Queenie can sense her sister's thoughts and feelings even from far away. When Tina is jailed in MACUSA awaiting execution, Queenie feels her sister's anguish and follows its mental trail to rescue her.

DRESSMAKING

Queenie's charms automate the tailoring process on her dressmaker's dummy.

YOUNGER-OLDER

Despite Queenie being the younger sister, she often acts as the older one, reminding Tina how to eat right and lecturing her on the pitfalls of her continued surveillance of the Second Salemers. Queenie is very protective of her sister.

LEGILIMENS

Queenie is a Legilimens: She has the ability to see inside another's mind and read his or her thoughts.

RELATIONSHIPS

JACOB KOWALSKI

Jacob and Queenie are different in many ways, but Queenie has no qualms about befriending a No-Maj with a good heart and honest intentions.

TINA GOLDSTEIN

Tina and Queenie are not only sisters—they are also best friends, coworkers, and roommates. Queenie and Tina may be different in some ways, but they acknowledge and respect each other's individual talents.

MRS. ESPOSITO

The landlady who rents the apartment to the Goldstein sisters has certain house rules. Before Tina brings Newt and Jacob inside the apartment, she warns them that she is not supposed to bring men onto the premises.

ABERNATHY

As the boss in charge of the Wand Permit Office at MACUSA, Abernathy is always asking Tina about Queenie's absences. Queenie is not a "career girl" like her sister, and tries to spend little time in the basement with her Wand Permit Office colleagues.

DEFINING MOMENTS

SUPPERTIME SURPRISE

Queenie and Tina are gracious hostesses, and conjure up a delicious dinner for themselves and their guests in no time flat. They even serve Jacob's favorite dessert, strudel.

PRISON BREAK

Queenie's Legilimens senses alert her to the fact that Tina is in trouble at MACUSA. She picks up her wand and storms into the Woolworth Building to come to her sister's rescue. While on the hunt for her sister, she saves Jacob from having his memory wiped.

JACOB KOWALSKI

NAME:
JACOB KOWALSKI

PROFESSION:
CANNING FACTORY WORKER/ ASPIRING BAKER

POLISH PIONEER

Jacob's family originally comes from Poland. Having recently returned to America's shores from Europe after serving in the Great War, he is eager to embark on a new adventure and become a self-made man, baking and selling Polish pastries.

CLOTHING & POSSESSIONS

Jacob's a stocky No-Maj, with a waistline that alludes to just how much he loves pastry. He keeps his curly brown hair slick and parted, and his thin mustache finely groomed. For his trip to secure a loan at Steen National Bank, Jacob wears an ill-fitted suit, hoping to make a good impression.

OVERCOAT

A classic woolen coat doubles as a suit jacket.

VEST

Buttoned almost to the point of bursting, Jacob wears a light gray vest under his dark overcoat.

SHIRT

A pale green dress shirt offsets the darker tones of Jacob's vest and coat.

SILVER EGG

Jacob meets Newt while they are sharing a bench at Steen National Bank. When Newt runs off to chase his escaped Niffler, Jacob notices that he left behind a small silver egg. Jacob sees the unusual egg and picks it up. Much to his surprise, the egg shakes in his hand, ready to hatch.

NECKTIE

Jacob chooses a red, polka-dotted tie.

CASE

Jacob owns a leather case that, from the outside, is virtually identical to the one Newt carries. Rather than keeping creatures in his case, however, Jacob uses his to carry pastries that he hopes will impress the bank manager.

SLACKS

Roomy but well-tailored pants match the color of Jacob's coat.

SHOES

Polished leather shoes complement the rest of Jacob's outfit.

CHARACTER PHILOSOPHY

AMERICAN DREAMER

Jacob wants to achieve his dreams as a professional baker.

FRESH FOODIE

Despite his big dreams, Jacob lives in a world where he can't seem to get ahead, no matter how hard he tries. He works a soul-sucking job at a factory canning preserved foods. He believes the best foods don't come out of a can, but use fresh ingredients, like the pastries he bakes.

> ## "I WANT TO MAKE PASTRY. IT MAKES PEOPLE HAPPY."
>
> –Jacob Kowalski

OPEN MIND

When Newt takes Jacob inside his case to see the beasts, Jacob stares at all the creatures in absolute wonder. Jacob is so open-minded and imaginative that he is able to accept what he sees before him.

COURAGE UNDER FIRE

Thrust suddenly into a strange world of magic and beasts, Jacob quivers and trembles at times, but he never runs away or gives up. It takes an extraordinary No-Maj to help apprehend a stampeding Erumpent—especially one that is in the middle of mating season.

SKILLS

Jacob may not have magical gifts, but he's accomplished in other areas that his new friends lack.

✳ ✳ ✳ ✳ ✳ ✳ ✳ 🦉 ✳ ✳ ✳ ✳ ✳ ✳ ✳

PASTRY PERFECTIONIST

Equipped with his grandmother's recipes and a pinch of "orange zest," Jacob Kowalski believes he makes the best *babka* and *pączki* pastries this side of Kraków. Unfortunately, the bank manager isn't willing to give them a try.

COOKING CHARISMA

Jacob is extremely impressed to see Queenie shares his love of extraordinary cooking and baking. This is just one of the many qualities he finds attractive about this amazing witch.

TOUGH NUT

Jacob may look harmless, but don't be fooled—he can knock a wizard on his backside when he needs to—just ask Newt!

BACKGROUND

WAR WEARY

During the Great War, Jacob joined the American Expeditionary Force and fought in Europe. He stayed on his birth continent for six years after the war, before deciding to travel back to America and start a new life.

FANGED FEAR

Jacob recoils when Newt introduces him to the three-headed serpentine Runespoor. Unlike the gentle Mooncalves, this beast is not one of Jacob's favorites.

DIRE STRAITS

Jacob dwells in a run-down tenement building in New York's Lower East Side. His meager homestead is in such bad shape that he has to enter the apartment by climbing in through the fire escape window.

MR. BINGLEY

Sweet pastries can't buy influence with the manager at Steen National Bank, Mr. Bingley. He views potential business loans in terms of profit and productivity, for which Jacob's application falls short.

FED-UP FIANCÉE

When Jacob cannot secure the loan for his bakery, Mildred, his fiancée, returns the engagement ring he gave her.

RELATIONSHIPS

QUEENIE GOLDSTEIN

Simply put, this captivating blond witch takes Jacob's breath away. Queenie's mutual interest in Jacob is a pleasant surprise, because many girls would find him rather unassuming. Yet Queenie sees beyond his bumbling exterior, into what lies beyond.

NEWT SCAMANDER

Jacob and Newt don't get off to the best start, with Jacob knocking Newt down and accidentally running off with the wrong leather case. The creatures that break loose from Newt's case, however, pull the two together under unlikely circumstances, and they form a strong bond of friendship.

DEFINING MOMENTS

BEAST BITTEN

Inadvertently swapping his case with Newt's, Jacob opens the case expecting to find his *pączki* pastries but instead, finds a beast—Newt's Murtlap. This rodent-like creature jumps out, and the resulting struggle between man and beast leaves Jacob with a bite wound on his neck and magical poison racing through his veins.

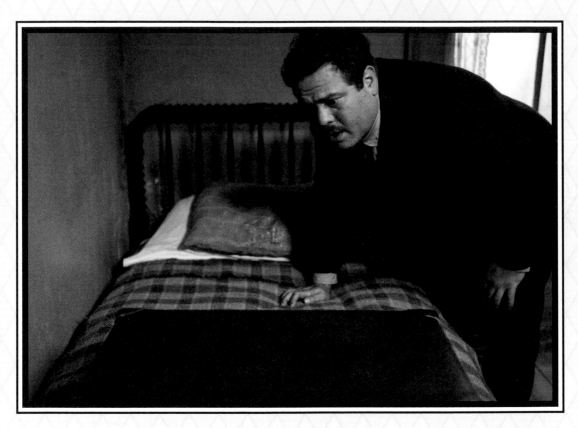

MATING SEASON

Newt's plan to bait the escaped Erumpent goes haywire when he mistakenly spills most of the beast's scent on Jacob. This musk was meant to attract and lure the beast back into Newt's case, but instead the female Erumpent is attracted to Jacob. She bolts after him, sending him on a mad dash for safety—up a tree!

EASY READ

Jacob is a gentleman. His thoughts, however, reveal a different side of him—which Queenie reacts to with a giggle. To Queenie, Jacob's mind is an open book, something he finds surprisingly refreshing.

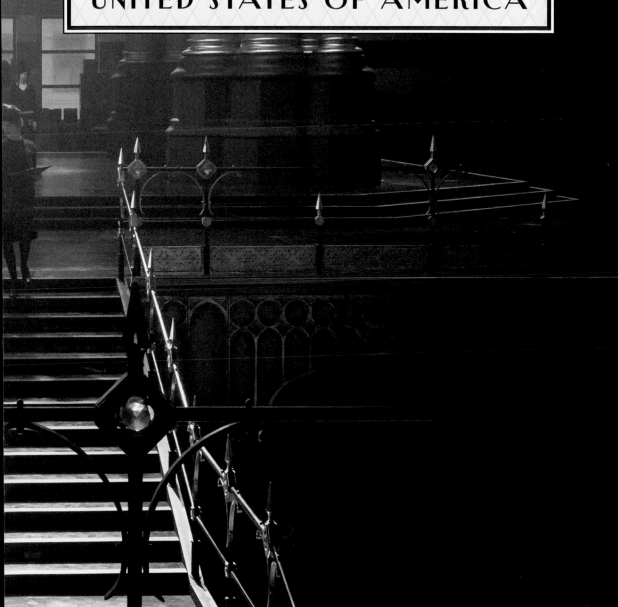

CHARACTER OVERVIEW

NAME:
SERAPHINA PICQUERY

PROFESSION:
PRESIDENT OF MACUSA

SCHOOLING:
ILVERMORNY SCHOOL OF WITCHCRAFT AND WIZARDRY

GRACE UNDER FIRE

Regal and powerful, President Picquery awes those who come to seek an audience with the Congress.

CLOTHING & POSSESSIONS

President Picquery wears ornate attire when she addresses the Congress.

PRESIDENTIAL HEADPIECE

President Picquery's golden floral headdress dazzles everyone who looks upon her.

PRESIDENTIAL GOWN

Gold embroiders the elegant black dress with a pattern that resembles the rays of the sun.

CHARACTER PHILOSOPHY

A few general principles guide President Picquery's administration.

LETTER OF THE LAW

President Picquery is strict when it comes to interpreting magical law. Those who break the law must be punished accordingly.

NO EXPOSURE

One of President Picquery's primary focuses is ensuring that the magical realm remains concealed from the No-Maj world.

KEEP THE PEACE

If the menace leaving a path of destruction throughout New York City is not stopped soon, the No-Majs may realize something supernatural is in their midst, which could reveal the existence of the wizarding world. President Picquery works hard to prevent this from happening, knowing a war between witches, wizards, and No-Majs would be devastating for everyone.

STRONG DEFENSE

In case of a war, President Picquery maintains a skilled company of wizards and witches who can repel a No-Maj attack and fight back if necessary.

CHARACTER OVERVIEW

NAME:
PERCIVAL GRAVES

PROFESSION:
DIRECTOR OF MAGICAL SECURITY AT MACUSA

COMMANDING PRESENCE

Graves projects an aura of authority and always seems to be in control of himself and his surroundings, no matter how chaotic things become.

> "YOU ARE AN INTERESTING MAN, MR. SCAMANDER. RATHER LIKE YOUR SUITCASE, I THINK THERE IS MUCH MORE TO YOU THAN MEETS THE EYE."
>
> –Percival Graves

CLOTHING & POSSESSIONS

Graves wears finely tailored clothes. One thing stands out about his wardrobe, as he prefers a single color for most of his clothing: black.

OVERCOAT

Graves wears a long dark coat with white piping and sleeves.

WAISTCOAT

Graves keeps his black waistcoat buttoned from top to bottom.

SHIRT

A white dress shirt adds contrast to the black shroud of Graves's outfit.

NECKTIE

Knotted tightly under Graves's collar, a black tie punctuates the wizard's look. Upon closer inspection, an onlooker may notice that Graves also dons two scorpion-shaped lapel pins to complement his intimidating exterior.

BOOTS

Black, leather, and polished to the point of reflection, Graves's boots never seem to get dirty.

DEATHLY HALLOWS NECKLACE

Graves has in his possession a pendant showing a circle bisected inside a triangle—the symbol of the Deathly Hallows.

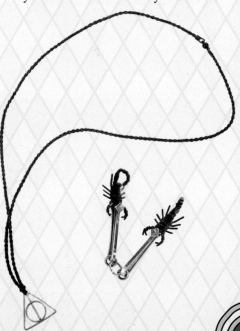

CHARACTER PHILOSOPHY

TRUTH DETECTIVE

Graves doesn't need to ask many questions to get the answers he wants. His eyes pierce and his mind probes, showing his skills as an expert interrogator.

ON THE HUNT

Graves believes that the path to the power he seeks can be found in a certain child with tremendous magical abilities. Graves's visions show that the child is close to the leader of the NSPS, Mary Lou Barebone. Graves enlists the help of Mary Lou's son, Credence, hoping he may hold the key to the child's secret identity.

> "CREDENCE—THERE IS NO NEED TO HIDE, NO NEED FOR SHAME. YOU AND I ARE THE SAME. WE'VE BOTH HAD TO HIDE WHAT WE WANT, AND WHO WE ARE."
>
> –Percival Graves

SECRET SPILLER

Graves has no misgivings about manipulating others to get his way. When interrogating Newt, he tries to use the Magizoologist's dismissal from Hogwarts to embarrass him, and shift the power dynamic between the two wizards into his favor.

FINGER POINTER

Graves accuses Newt of being sent to New York by Albus Dumbledore, an acclaimed wizard and teacher at Hogwarts. He claims that Newt set his beasts loose in New York on purpose in order to expose the wizarding world, and provoke war between the magical and non-magical worlds.

BACKGROUND

MAN OF MYSTERY

Graves has the trust of the wizarding community, and uses this to his advantage. He can play his opponents accordingly and angle for what he needs.

CHILD SEEKER

Graves knows that Mary Lou is close to the child he wants to find, so he reaches out to her adopted son, Credence, for help. Graves thinks that Credence is a Squib, a person who is non-magical but has at least one magical parent, and that this could help in his search.

> ## "I CAN TELL YOU THAT HE OR SHE IS NO OLDER THAN TEN. I SAW THEM IN CLOSE PROXIMITY TO YOUR MOTHER. SHE, I SAW PLAINLY."
>
> –Percival Graves

TWO FACED

Graves accuses Newt of trying to intentionally reveal the wizarding world, but Graves himself admits to Credence that he doesn't want to live in the shadows of hidden magic forever.

R E L A T I O N S H I P S

SERAPHINA PICQUERY

The President of MACUSA depends on Graves for his wise counsel and skill. He has made himself indispensable both to Picquery and, by extension, to the organization as a whole.

NEWT SCAMANDER

Graves is suspicious of Newt from the very beginning because of the Magizoologist's ties to Albus Dumbledore. Graves does not trust Dumbledore or his intentions, and he suspects that the great wizard sent Newt to New York for some greater purpose.

CREDENCE BAREBONE

Graves sees Credence as a tool he can manipulate for his powers of perception in the magical realm.

ALBUS DUMBLEDORE

Graves reveals during Newt's interrogation that he knows Dumbledore argued against Newt's expulsion from Hogwarts. He makes it clear that he questions Dumbledore's motives.

DEFINING MOMENTS

SILENT OBSERVER

Hiding in plain sight among journalists and photographers, Graves witnesses firsthand how the Obscurus lays waste to a city street.

INQUISITIVE INTERROGATOR

Before Newt and Tina face execution, Graves enters their cell to find out more about the Obscurus that is wreaking havoc through New York.

MAGICAL MOMENT

While having a secret meeting at a diner with Credence, Graves turns an ordinary, wilted carnation into a Periculid, a beautiful but deadly magical flower.

THE INTERNATIONAL CONFEDERATION

MACUSA representatives and delegates from the International Confederation convene in the Pentagram Office with President Picquery to discuss matters of international importance.

"THE INTERNATIONAL CONFEDERATION IS THREATENING TO SEND A DELEGATION. THEY THINK THIS MIGHT BE RELATED TO GRINDELWALD'S ATTACKS IN EUROPE."

–President Picquery

COMMITTEE PROBE

The international delegates join in President Picquery's questioning of Newt Scamander. While all listen intently to the interrogation, none speak out in the Magizoologist's defense, or in agreement with Newt's assertion that an Obscurus, not his escaped creatures, are behind the strange occurrences in New York.

MACUSA EMPLOYEES

NAME: RANJIT
PROFESSION: MACUSA AUROR

Ranjit is one of President Picquery's handpicked investigators.
She tasks him with investigating the root cause of the disturbances
in New York City.

NAME: RED THE DWARF
PROFESSION: MACUSA ELEVATOR ATTENDANT

Red owes his name to his scruffy red hair and beard. He is the elevator
operator at MACUSA, helping the wizards and witches reach their
intended destinations. Despite his small stature, he has no problem with
the controls, using a clawed stick to tap buttons too high for him to reach
by hand.

NAME: BERYL
PROFESSION: MACUSA STAFF

Beryl has found that following the lives of witches and wizards is far more
enjoyable than being one. On any given day, she can be found in the
MACUSA basement, avoiding work while reading a magazine.

NAME: ABERNATHY
PROFESSION: HEAD OF WAND PERMIT
OFFICE AT MACUSA

Though he's nearly the same age as Tina Goldstein, and younger than some of the other workers who labor in his office, Abernathy insists that his subordinates all refer to him as "sir."

NAME: SAM
PROFESSION: MACUSA OBLIVIATOR

Even though he's an Obliviator, work is rarely the foremost thing on Sam's mind. He would much rather entertain witches by taking them to his private booth at the Scalded Dragon. Sam is quick to flash his handsome mug at those whose hearts he might later break.

MACUSA
DEPARTMENTS

MACUSA contains many different departments
of witches and wizards.

AURORS

Aurors constitute the authoritative force of MACUSA. They investigate
cases concerning magic used for dark purposes, and bring any culprits to
the Congress for reckoning.

EXECUTIONERS

Executioners obey the will of the Congress and terminate the lives of witches and wizards who have committed serious or dangerous crimes.

OBLIVIATORS

Obliviators help keep the wizarding world secret by erasing the memories of No-Majs who witness magical acts. They also do the same to rogue wizards.

EXTERMINATORS

The combat troops of MACUSA, Exterminators are ready for action at a moment's notice. They are tasked with hunting down fantastic creatures and corrupt wizards.

HEALERS

When basic medicine and healing potions aren't enough, witches and wizards turn to MACUSA's Healers, first-rate caregivers with deep knowledge of curative spells.

THE SECOND SALEMERS

CHARACTER OVERVIEW

NAME:
MARY LOU BAREBONE

PROFESSION:
NSPS SOCIETY LEADER

✳ ✳ ✳ ✳ ✳ ✳ ✳ ❦ ✳ ✳ ✳ ✳ ✳ ✳ ✳

NO FRILLS

A severe woman, Mary Lou adorns herself with the plainest of clothes and forsakes all other earthly comforts for the good of her cause.

NSPS

Mary Lou heads the New Salem Philanthropic Society, whose chief goal is to invoke a "Second Salem," a new round of witchcraft trials. Her goal is to uncover—and exterminate—those living in their midst who are concealing magical powers.

MOTHER FIGURE

Mary Lou has adopted three orphans—Credence, Chastity, and Modesty—and feeds countless other children at her old church. Her benevolence comes at a price: These children are tasked with spreading the NSPS's message all over the city.

"LISTEN TO ME, FRIENDS, AND LAUGH IF YOU DARE: WITCHES LIVE AMONG US!"

–Mary Lou Barebone

NAME:
CREDENCE BAREBONE

PROFESSION:
NSPS ACOLYTE

PAMPHLETEER

Credence roams the city every day, distributing NSPS pamphlets to anyone willing to take one. But Credence has another job, too. He is secretly assisting Graves in his search to find a mysterious, powerful child with an unknown purpose.

CORPORAL PUNISHMENT

Mary Lou suspects that her son is not always telling her the truth about his whereabouts. Her disciplinary measures can be quite severe as she tries to exert control over him.

SPECIAL BOY

Mary Lou tells Credence his birth mother was "a wicked and unnatural woman," implying that he may share the same qualities. Senator Shaw calls Credence a "freak show." Only Graves accepts Credence as he is, seeing the boy for his full potential.

NAME:
CHASTITY BAREBONE

PROFESSION:
NSPS ACOLYTE

PURE OF HEART

Chastity follows the example of her adopted mother, Mary Lou, by refusing to indulge in anything that could lead her down a dark path. Despite her austere exterior, Chastity is genuinely kind and compassionate, and cares deeply for others.

LOYAL DAUGHTER

One of Chastity's main responsibilities is dishing out gruel to the many children who come to the NSPS church looking for a handout.

CHARACTER OVERVIEW

NAME:
MODESTY BAREBONE

PROFESSION:
NSPS ACOLYTE

＊ ＊ ＊ ＊ ＊ ＊ ❤ ＊ ＊ ＊ ＊ ＊ ＊ ＊

CURIOUS CHILD

Modesty knows what she should and should not do according to her strict mother, Mary Lou. But sometimes Modesty feels compelled to go against her mother, such as when she borrows a toy magic wand from a friend to play with in secret.

THE SHAW
FAMILY

CHARACTER OVERVIEW

NAME:
HENRY SHAW SR.

PROFESSION:
NEWSPAPER MAGNATE AND PRESIDENT OF SHAW ENTERPRISES

✳ ✳ ✳ ✳ ✳ ✳ 🦉 ✳ ✳ ✳ ✳ ✳ ✳

SHAW ENTERPRISES

At Shaw Towers in Manhattan, Henry Shaw Sr. runs the media corporation, Shaw Enterprises. His major newspapers—the *New York Clarion*, *Washington Enquirer*, and *Massachusetts Herald*—give him the opportunity to influence millions of readers.

NIGHT ON THE TOWN

When his son and namesake, Senator Shaw, hosts a benefit dinner to fund his reelection campaign, Henry Shaw Sr. is quick to lend his support.

CHARACTER OVERVIEW

NAME:
SENATOR HENRY SHAW JR.

PROFESSION:
UNITED STATES SENATOR

CAREER POLITICIAN
Suave and clean-cut, Henry Shaw Jr. is the consummate politician, ready to win over anyone he meets.

GOLDEN BOY
Henry Shaw is the older of the Shaw brothers, and also the more successful—at least, in their father's estimation. Both father and son share a love of power and a no-nonsense attitude about getting a job done.

CHARACTER OVERVIEW

NAME:
LANGDON SHAW

PROFESSION:
UNKNOWN

SECOND-CLASS CITIZEN

No one in the Shaw family pays Langdon any serious attention, and as a result, he becomes very jealous of his father and brother's close relationship. In an effort to gain favor, Langdon brings members of the NSPS to his father's suite in Shaw Towers. He thinks what the NSPS members have to say is newsworthy, but his father views this as a disappointment and waste of time.

"THOSE CRAZY DISTURBANCES IN THE SUBWAY—LOOK AT THESE PICTURES! DO YOU SEE IT? IT'S EXACTLY LIKE WHAT THE WITNESSES HAVE BEEN DESCRIBING!"

–Langdon Shaw

NAME:
GNARLAK

PROFESSION:
OWNER OF THE BLIND PIG

STREETWISE

Gnarlak strives to know everything that's happening on either side of the law. Information is Gnarlak's true trade—and as long as the price is right, Gnarlak is as reliable a source as they come.

BLIND EYE

Those who patronize The Blind Pig are often thirsty for more than a drink. Many witches and wizards come to play cards and illegally gamble money and magical artifacts. Gnarlak knows all about what goes on his establishment, and uses this knowledge to his advantage.

"YOU'VE GOT A BIG PRICE ON YOUR HEAD, MR. SCAMANDER. WHY SHOULD I HELP YOU INSTEAD OF TURNIN' YOU IN?"

–Gnarlak

THE BLIND PIG

This is a rough place filled with the saltiest of witches and wizards, many of them outlaws. They each have unique talents, but all enjoy the gigglewater and music The Blind Pig has to offer.

THE
OBSCURUS

THE NEW YORK GHOST

VOL. LXIII NO. 190871 - DAILY · MONDAY 6TH DECEMBER 1926 · PRICE 0.03 DRAGOTS

MAGICAL DISTURBANCES RISK WIZARDING EXPOSURE

PRESIDENT SERAPHINA PICQUERY TO ADDRESS FEARFUL AMERICAN WIZARDING COMMUNITY

Thousands of letters will be dispatched across America from tomorrow. Owls on stand by.

by E.L. Piltsus

CULTURE
SECTION 4 — PAGE 7 AND 8

WIZZJAZZ TAKES NEW YORK BY STORM
Music — page 7 1/2

Revered tome "Big Foot Last Stand" gets Wizard Broadway adaptation
W Lemus reports

SPORTS
SECTION 4 — PAGE 7 AND 8

WIZARDS INTRIGUED YET FASCINATED BY NO-MAJ 'BASEBALL'
E. Laushini Investigations

Fitchburg Finches scores high at the USA Quidditch League
Quidditch Corner - pg 7

WIZBIZ
SECTION 3 — PAGE 13

Dragots value hit by low potions exports
by M. Carneirus

MACUSA ON MAXIMUM ALERT - FULL REPORT PG.13

● *International Confederation of Wizards called for emergency meeting. Pgs 15/17*

MACUSA HEADQUARTERS - NYC.

What is this perplexing sinister aura?

KOREAN MASTER AUROLOGISTS DRAFTED IN FOR CONJECTURE

NEW YORK and SEOUL.

by C. Williamsum

HUNDREDS OF FORGED WAND PERMITS INTERCEPTED. A CONNECTION WITH CURRENT UNEXPLAINABLE EVENTS?
Editor's Comment

GELLERT GRINDELWALD INTERNATIONAL WIZARD HUNT INTENSIFIES

NEW YORK, PARIS, LONDON AND CASABLANCA.

THE MIDWEST ASSOCIATION OF WARLOCKS & WITCHES QUESTIONING MACUSA'S DEFENSE EFFORTS

CHICAGO, ILLINOIS.

"WITCHES LIVE AMONG US!"
No-Majes consider Second Salemers' claim. Further threat to wizarding secrecy?

by M.P. Nettum

No-Maj Holiday Season threatened by mysterious explosions. Panic soars.

by M.L. Miraphorum

No-Maj Borough - New Jersey.

THE MACUSA INDEX OF MAGICAL EXPOSURE THREAT — No.50.26

Data provided by the Surveillance Dept.

NEW YORK CITY.

Suspicious Wizards questioned by MACUSA officials

by R. Pukanhouse

MACUSA HEADQUARTERS - NYC.

L M I H D E

DANGER
L. LOW THREAT, M. MODERATE THREAT, I. IMMINENT THREAT,
H. HIGH ALERT, D. DANGER, E. EMERGENCY.

EDITORIAL
by E.L. Piltsus

OVERVIEW

MYSTERIOUS HAPPENINGS

The Obscurus manifests itself primarily through destructive actions. Many dismiss it as pure "atmospheric hooey" or some kind of electrical storm. Yet those who glimpse or hear the Obscurus's physical form liken it to a snarling, shadowy cloud with eyes.

EARTH SHAKER

As it flies through the street, the Obscurus rattles manhole covers, breaks windows, topples lampposts, and sends pedestrians flying. It causes major destruction throughout the city.

RALLY RIOT

Senator Shaw's political fund-raiser goes terribly awry when the Obscurus charges inside.

WITNESS: "AND IT WAS LIKE A . . ."

REPORTER: "LIKE A WIND OR LIKE A . . ."

WITNESS: "LIKE A GHOST, BUT DARK . . . AND I SAW ITS EYES. SHINY WHITE EYES."

BACKGROUND

POWER STRUGGLE

During the witch hunts in centuries past, young witches and wizards sometimes tried to suppress their magic to avoid persecution. The unused energy created an unstable, uncontrollable, dark force inside the child. Like a parasite, it would drain the child's power and ultimately their life force.

SHORT LIFE SPAN

The Obscurus consumes so much energy that the host child typically doesn't live to be more than ten years old.

COMPLETE CONTROL

President Picquery and the International Confederation cannot fathom there could be an Obscurial in the United States, or anywhere for that matter.

LIVING IN A BOX

Newt knows that Obscurials still exist. He encountered one recently in Sudan, Africa. He found a young girl who had been shut away by her tribe because she showed signs of magic. The Obscurus was taking her over, depleting her strength, and killing her. Newt was able to separate the Obscurus from the child just before she died. He trapped it inside a shimmering black box and put it inside his case so he could study it. Newt insists that without the host child, this Obscurus is harmless.

BEASTS

ERUMPENT

NIFFLER

BOWTRUCKLE

BILLYWIG

OCCAMY

DEMIGUISE

MURTLAP

DOXY

BONUS FEATURE

THE ART OF

FANTASTIC BEASTS

AND WHERE TO FIND THEM™

PORPENTINA GOLDSTEIN

PERCIVAL GRAVES

FANTASTIC BEASTS
AND WHERE TO FIND THEM